After-School Snacks

kids cook!

Company's Coming

KIDS COOK SERIES

After-School Snacks

Copyright © Company's Coming Publishing Limited

Published by
Company's Coming U.S.A., L.C. © 2005
Maitland, Florida, USA 32751
Tel: 407-916-1950
Fax: 407-916-0600

Printed in the United States of America

Table of Contents

kids cook!

Kids Cook! cookbooks provide the necessary tools to teach your child the basics of cooking in a way that is fun and easy.

Helping your child learn to cook has many benefits and rewards:

- Cooking is a great family activity that will create memories that will last a lifetime.

- Cooking makes kids more confident, self-sufficient and independent.

- Cooking helps children develop skills such as counting, decision-making, measuring and creativity.

- Cooking encourages a greater appreciation of mealtime and openness toward new and varied foods (kids will eat their own creations).

- Cooking with kids helps Mom with family meal planning and preparation.

Collect all 3 cookbooks in the Kids Cook! Series:
Bag Lunches
After-School Snacks
Weekend Treats

All *Kids Cook!* cookbooks feature:
- Step-by-step instructions
- Everyday ingredients
- Kitchen-tested recipes

Bring out the chef in your child and let your kids cook today!

Foreword

Your biggest hunger gap of the day—after school and before supper! Why not make a delicious snack to tide you over. Choose one of these specially selected recipes from the Company's Coming family of cookbooks. Everything you could want to munch on is here: dips, drinks, hot and cold finger food, sweet treats, and more!

Before you get started, check out the Get Ready section of each recipe. Every utensil and piece of equipment you will need is listed in the order you will use it. Line them up as listed and you will have what you need when you need it! A picture dictionary of all the equipment and utensils can be found on pages 8 and 9. Any Cooking Terms you might not know are explained on pages 6 and 7.

And remember, there is always that one important last step. Clean up the kitchen when you've finished making your snack! It will make supper preparations that much quicker and more enjoyable for the main cook in your family.

Safety

1. Never touch anything electrical with your wet hands.
2. Always pull out a plug by holding and pulling on the plug itself, not the cord.
3. Keep saucepan handles turned inward on top of the stove.
4. Know how to properly use all appliances before starting. (Ask Mom or Dad if you're not sure.)
5. Handle hot plates and dishes with well-insulated oven mitts.
6. Turn off burners and oven, and unplug small appliances when not in use.

A note to parents:

This book is intended for your children to use. It has been especially written for kids aged 8 to 15 years. Please supervise them when necessary. The handling of sharp knives, boiling liquids, and hot pans needs to be monitored carefully with younger children.

Cooking Terms

Bake
To cook in an oven preheated to the temperature it says in the recipe. Use either the bottom or center rack.

Batter
A mixture of flour, liquid and other ingredients that can be thin (such as pancake batter) or thick (such as muffin batter).

Beat
To mix two or more ingredients with a spoon, fork or electric mixer, using a circular motion.

Blend
To mix two or more ingredients with a spoon, fork, electric mixer or electric blender until combined.

Boil
To heat a liquid in a saucepan until bubbles rise in a steady pattern and break on the surface. Steam also starts to rise from the surface.

Break An Egg
Tap the side of an egg on the edge of a bowl or cup to crack the shell. Place the tips of both thumbs in the crack and open the shell, letting the egg yolk and egg white drop into the bowl.

Broil
To cook under the top heating element in the oven. Use either the top rack or the upper rack.

Chill
To place in the refrigerator until cold.

Chop
To cut food into small pieces with a sharp knife on a cutting board; to chop finely is to cut foods as small as you can.

Combine
To put two or more ingredients together.

Cream
To beat an ingredient or combination of ingredients until the mixture is soft, smooth and "creamy," using a spoon or electric mixer.

Cut In
To combine butter or margarine with dry ingredients (such as flour) using a fork or pastry blender until the mixture looks like big crumbs the size of green peas.

Dice
To cut food into small ¼ inch cube-shaped pieces.

Drain
To strain away an unwanted liquid (such as water, fruit juice or grease) using a colander or strainer. Drain water or juice over the kitchen sink or in a bowl. Drain grease into a metal can, chill until hardened, then throw away in the garbage.

Drizzle
To dribble drops or lines of glaze or icing over food in a random manner from tines of a fork or the tip of a spoon.

6

Fold

To mix gently, using a rubber spatula, by cutting down in the center and lifting towards the edge of the bowl. Use a "down, up, over" movement, turning the bowl as you repeat.

Garnish

To decorate food with edible condiments such as parsley sprigs, fruit slices or vegetable cut-outs.

Heat

To make something warm or hot by placing the saucepan on the stove burner that is turned on to the level it says in the recipe.

Knead

To work dough into a smooth putty-like mass by pressing and folding using the heels of your hands.

Let Stand

To let a baked product cool slightly on a wire rack or hot pad, while still in its baking pan. Also, any other mixture that requires time to sit on the counter for the flavors to blend.

Mash

To squash cooked or very ripe foods with a fork or potato masher.

Melt

To heat a solid food (such as butter, margarine, cheese or chocolate) until it turns into a liquid. Be careful not to burn it.

Mix

(see Combine)

Mixing Just Until Moistened

To stir dry ingredients with liquid ingredients until dry ingredients are barely wet. Mixture will still be lumpy.

Process

To mix or cut up food in a blender (or food processor) until it is the way it says in the recipe.

Sauté

To cook food quickly in a small amount of oil in a frying pan, wok, or special sauté pan over medium heat.

Scramble-Fry

To brown ground meat in hot oil using a spoon, fork or pancake lifter to break up the meat into small crumb-like pieces as it cooks.

Scrape (Scraping down the sides)

To use a rubber spatula to remove as much of a mixture as possible from inside a bowl or saucepan.

Simmer

To heat liquids in a saucepan on low on the stove burner so that small bubbles appear on the surface around the sides of the liquid.

Slice

To cut foods such as apples, carrots, tomatoes, meat or bread into thin sections or pieces, using a sharp knife.

Spoon (into)

Using a spoon to scoop ingredients from one container to another.

Spread

To cover the surface of one product (generally a more solid food such as bread) with another product (generally a softer food such as icing or butter).

Stir

To mix two or more ingredients with a spoon, using a circular motion.

Stir-Fry

To heat food quickly in a frying pan on medium-high stirring constantly.

Toast

To brown slightly in a toaster, frying pan, or under the broiler in the oven.

Toss

To mix salad or other ingredients gently with a lifting motion, using two forks, two spoons or salad tongs.

7

Equipment & Utensils

Barbecue fork

Blender

Baking sheet

Bread knife

Casserole dish

Colander

Cookie sheet

Cutting board

Dry measures

Frying pan

Hot pad

Electric mixer

Electric frying pan

Ice-cream scoop

Liquid measures

Mixing spoons

Measuring spoons

Loaf pan

Muffin pan

Bowls (mixing)

Oblong baking dish

Oblong baking pan

Oven mitts

Parfait spoon

Pancake lifter

Pastry brush

Pastry blender

Pie plate

Pizza pan

Rubber spatula

Rolling pin

Potato masher

Round cake pan

Square baking pan

Saucepan

Sharp knife

Sieve or strainer

Table knife, fork & spoon

Tube pan

Burners

Top Rack

Center Rack

Upper Rack

Bottom Rack

Oven with rack positions

Whisk

Wire rack

Tongs

9

Lemon Cola Float

GET READY ✔
liquid measures, drinking glass, ice-cream scoop

| 1. | Cola soft drink, chilled | 1 cup |
| | Scoops of lemon sherbet | 2 |

1. Pour the soft drink into the glass. Add the lemon sherbet. Makes 1 float.

The perfect beverage to treat yourself to after school.

Peach Melba Float

GET READY ✔
blender, 3 drinking glasses, liquid measures, mixing spoon, ice-cream scoop

1. Can of sliced peaches, with juice   **14 oz.**
2. Ginger ale   **2¼ cups**
3. Scoops of raspberry sherbet   **3**

1. Put the peach slices into the blender. Place the lid on the blender. Process on high for 15 seconds or until smooth. Divide among the 3 glasses.
2. Pour ¾ cup (175 mL) ginger ale into each glass. Stir.
3. Add 1 scoop of the raspberry sherbet to each glass. Serve immediately. Makes 3 floats.

These flavors explode in your mouth.

Root Beer Float/Soda

GET READY ✔
ice-cream scoop, drinking glass, long-handled spoon

1. **Rounded scoops of vanilla ice cream**   2
   Chilled root beer, to fill the glass

1. Put the ice cream into the drinking glass.
   Pour the root beer over the ice cream to
   fill the glass. Makes 1 large drink.

Variation: Use any other flavor of your favorite
soft drink.

Whether you call this a float
or a soda, it is a cinch to
make any flavor you want.
Do not freeze.

Banana Berry Yogurt Shake

1.	Plain yogurt	1 cup
	Liquid or creamed honey	¼ cup
	Banana	1
	Prepared orange juice	½ cup
2.	Large frozen strawberries	6

1. Put the first 4 ingredients into the blender. Place the lid on the blender. Process for 30 seconds or until the banana is smooth.

2. While the blender is processing, add the strawberries, 1 at a time, through the opening in the lid. Process until smooth. Makes 1 large shake.

Front: Banana Berry Yogurt Shake, above

Great for a cold winter warm-up after school.

Hot Chocolate For One

GET READY ✔
measuring spoons, 12 oz. microwave-safe mug, liquid measures, mixing spoon

1.	Cocoa powder	**1 tbsp**
	Granulated sugar	**1 tbsp.**
2.	Water	**¾ cup**
3.	Skim evaporated milk	**⅔ cup**
4.	Vanilla flavoring	**¾ tsp.**
	Miniature marshmallows, for garnish	

1. Combine the cocoa powder and sugar in the mug.

2. Put the water in the 1 cup liquid measure. Microwave on high (100%) for 1½ minutes or until it boils. Pour the hot water slowly into the cocoa mixture. Stir until smooth.

3. Pour the evaporated milk into the same liquid measure. Microwave on high (100%) for 1 minute. Pour the warm milk into the mug.

4. Add the vanilla. Stir well. Place the marshmallows on top. Serves 1.

Strawberry Pineapple Cooler

1. Pineapple juice, chilled — 1 cup
   Skim milk powder — 2 tbsp.
   Large frozen strawberries — 3

2. Ginger ale (or club soda), optional — ½ cup

1. Combine the pineapple juice and milk powder in the blender. Place the lid on the blender. Process for 10 seconds. While the blender is processing, add the strawberries, 1 at a time, through the opening in the lid. Process until smooth.

2. Add the ginger ale to have a fizzy cooler. Stir. Makes 1⅓ cups.

BLUEBERRY PINEAPPLE COOLER: Follow the directions as above, substituting ½ cup frozen blueberries for the strawberries.

Pictured on this page.

A lovely deep mauve with a light mauve foam on top. The soft drink adds a little fizz.

Add a selection of veggies to round out a healthy snack.

Dill Dip

GET READY ✔

dry measures, measuring spoons, small bowl, mixing spoon

1.	Salad dressing (or mayonnaise)	⅔ cup
	Sour cream	⅔ cup
	Onion flakes	2 tsp.
	Parsley flakes	2 tsp.
	Dill weed	2 tsp.
	Paprika	¼ tsp.
	Celery salt	¼ tsp.

1. Combine all 7 ingredients in the bowl. Mix well. Makes about 1½ cups dip.

Spread on bread, bagels or crackers. Store any remaining spread in a covered container in the refrigerator for up to 3 days.

Smoked Salmon Spread

GET READY ✔

small bowl, table fork, dry measures, measuring spoons, mixing spoon

1.		
Can of salmon, well drained	7½ oz.
Plain spreadable cream cheese	⅓ cup
Finely chopped celery	1 tbsp.
Prepared horseradish	½ tsp.
Liquid smoke flavoring	⅛ tsp.
Onion powder	⅛ tsp.

1. Mash the salmon in the bowl with the fork. Add the remaining 5 ingredients. Mix well. Makes 1 cup spread.

Spread on graham crackers, digestive biscuits or any other whole wheat or whole grain cracker.

Choco Nut Spread

GET READY ✔

dry measures, liquid measures, measuring spoons, small bowl, mixing spoon

1.	**Smooth peanut butter**	**½ cup**
	Chocolate syrup	**⅓ cup**
	Vanilla flavoring	**1 tsp.**

1.   Combine all 3 ingredients in the bowl. Mix until smooth. Makes ¾ cup spread.

Taffy Fruit Dip

GET READY ✔

dry measures, measuring spoons, medium bowl, electric mixer, mixing spoon

1. Cream cheese, softened   **4 oz.**
   Brown sugar, packed   **½ cup**
   Vanilla flavoring   **2 tsp.**

2. Chopped peanuts (optional)   **¼ cup**
   Fresh fruit, for dipping

1. Beat the first 3 ingredients in the bowl with the mixer on medium speed until smooth and fluffy and the brown sugar is dissolved.

2. Stir in the peanuts. Dip the fresh fruit into the taffy dip. Chill any remaining dip. It will stiffen slightly. Soften in the microwave oven on low (20%) for just a few seconds. Makes ¾ cup dip.

   Pictured on page 19.

Honey Lime Fruit Dip

GET READY ✔

dry measures, measuring spoons, small bowl, mixing spoon

1. Sour cream (or thick plain yogurt)   **1 cup**
   Liquid honey   **2 tbsp.**
   Grated peel and juice of 1 medium lime
   Poppy seeds (optional)   **½ tsp.**

1. Combine all 4 ingredients in the bowl. Mix well. Chill for 5 minutes to blend the flavors. Makes 1 cup dip.

   Pictured on page 19.

Clockwise From Top Right: Taffy Fruit Dip, page 18, Honey Lime Fruit Dip, page 18, Honey Mustard Dip, below

Honey Mustard Dip

GET READY ✔
dry measures, measuring spoons, small bowl, mixing spoon

1. Sour cream   ½ cup
    Liquid honey   1 tbsp
    Prepared mustard   2 tsp.

1. Combine all 3 ingredients in the bowl. Mix well. Makes ½ cup dip.

This will become a favorite in your home.

Whole Wheat Crazy Bread

GET READY ✔

12 inch pizza pan or 10 × 15 inch baking sheet, measuring spoons, dry measures, 2 small bowls, mixing spoon, liquid measures, medium bowl, whisk, tea towel, sharp knife, pastry brush, oven mitts, wire rack

1.	Instant yeast	1 tbsp.
	Whole wheat flour	1 cup
2.	Very warm water	1 cup
	Cooking oil	1 tbsp.
	Granulated sugar	1 tsp.
	Salt	1 tsp.
3.	All-purpose flour	1½ cups
4.	Hard margarine, melted	2 tbsp.
	Garlic powder	⅛ tsp.
	Dried sweet basil	1 tsp.
5.	Grated Parmesan cheese	2 tbsp.

1. Place the oven rack in the center position. Turn the oven on to 400°F. Grease the pan. Combine the yeast and whole wheat flour in the one small bowl. Set aside.

2. Combine the water, cooking oil, sugar and salt in the medium bowl. Stir until dissolved. Add the whole wheat flour mixture. Whisk until smooth.

3. Add the all-purpose flour. Mix well. Cover the bowl with the tea towel. Let stand for 15 minutes.

4. Combine the margarine, garlic powder and basil in the second small bowl. Knead the flour mixture 3 or 4 times. Press out evenly in the greased pan. Cut into 14 sticks or fingers with the sharp knife. Brush the margarine mixture over the surface of the dough.

5. Sprinkle with the Parmesan cheese. Cover the baking sheet with the tea towel. Let stand for 15 minutes. Bake, uncovered, in the oven for 20 minutes or until lightly golden. Use the oven mitts to remove the pan to the wire rack to cool. Makes 14 crazy bread sticks.

Crunchy Maple Yogurt

GET READY ✔

dry measures, medium microwave-safe bowl, waxed paper, 2 mixing spoons, oven mitts, hot pad, measuring spoons, small bowl, 2 dessert bowls, covered container

1. CRUMBLE TOPPING

Hard margarine	¼ cup
Rolled oats (not instant)	¾ cup
Brown sugar, packed	¼ cup
Graham cracker crumbs	¼ cup
Long thread or fancy flake coconut	¼ cup

2. MAPLE YOGURT

Plain yogurt	8 oz.
Liquid honey	2 tsp.
Maple flavoring	¼ tsp.

1. **Crumble Topping:** Put the margarine into the microwave-safe bowl. Cover with the waxed paper. Microwave on high (100%) for 30 seconds. Add the next 4 ingredients. Mix well. Microwave on high (100%) for 30 seconds or until nicely toasted. Use the oven mitts to remove the bowl to the hot pad. Break up the mixture as it cools.

2. **Maple Yogurt:** Mix all 3 ingredients in the small bowl. Divide between the 2 dessert bowls and sprinkle each with the Crumble Topping. Store any remaining topping in a covered container in the refrigerator. Serves 2.

Crumble Topping is great to sprinkle over yogurt, fruit or pudding.

Fruity Chicken Pitas

1. Diced cooked chicken (or turkey)   1 cup
   Small apple, cored and diced   1
   Can of pineapple tidbits, well drained 8 oz.
   Crushed potato chips   1 cup

2. Salad dressing (or mayonnaise)   ½ cup
   Raisins   5 tbsp.
   Ground cinnamon   ¼ tsp.
   Chopped walnuts (optional)   2 tbsp.

3. Mini pita breads   10

1. Combine the first 4 ingredients in the medium bowl. Stir.

2. Combine the next 4 ingredients in the small bowl. Stir. Fold the salad dressing mixture into the chicken mixture with the rubber spatula until coated.

3. Carefully slit each pita bread open at one end with the knife. Fill each pita "pocket" with ¼ cup mixture. Makes 2½ cups, enough for 10 pitas.

Store leftover filling in the refrigerator for 2 to 3 days.

Salad Envelopes

GET READY ✔
sharp knife, cutting board, paper towel, table spoon, dry measures, medium bowl, mixing spoon, measuring spoons, 2 paper towels

1.	**Medium tomato**	**1**
2.	**Grated carrot**	**¼ cup**
	Green onion, thinly sliced	**1**
	Thinly sliced green, red or yellow pepper (2 inches long)	**¼ cup**
	Grated Cheddar cheese	**1 cup**
3.	**Creamy dressing (your favorite)**	**2 tbsp.**
	Shredded iceberg lettuce	**⅔ cup**
	White (or whole wheat) flour tortillas (10 inch size)	**2**

1. Cut the tomato in half with the knife on the cutting board. Gently squeeze over the paper towel to remove the seeds. Use the table spoon to scoop out the rest. Throw away the seeds and juice. Dice the tomato into 1 inch chunks on the cutting board.

2. Combine the tomato with the carrot, green onion, green pepper and cheese in the bowl. Stir.

3. Add the dressing. Toss the mixture to coat. Spread ½ of the lettuce down the middle of each tortilla. Spread ½ of the veggie mixture over the lettuce. Fold the bottom edge of the tortilla up over the filling to the center. Fold the left side over the center. Fold the right side overlapping the left side. Wrap in the paper towels to eat. Makes 2 envelopes.

A salad you can eat with your fingers.

Great for a fast after-school snack.

Peanut Butter Log

GET READY ✔
measuring spoons, small bowl, mixing spoon, table knife, waxed paper

1.	Smooth or chunky peanut butter	2 tbsp.
	Cream cheese, softened (or spreadable fruit-flavored cream cheese)	1 tbsp.
2.	White (or whole wheat) flour tortilla (10 inch size)	1
3.	Medium carrot, grated	1
	Light raisins	2 tbsp.

1. Use the spoon to cream the peanut butter and cream cheese together in the bowl.

2. Use the knife to spread the peanut butter mixture on one side of the tortilla.

3. Sprinkle the carrot and raisins over the peanut butter. Press down with your hand. Roll the tortilla up like a jelly roll. Wrap one end with the waxed paper and eat with your hands. Makes 1 log.

Fruit Roll Tortillas

1.	**Cream cheese, softened**	**4 oz.**
2.	**Icing (confectioner's) sugar**	**2 tbsp.**
	Can of crushed pineapple, well drained	**8 oz.**
	(see Tip)	
	Long thread coconut	**¼ cup**
3.	**White (or whole wheat) flour tortillas**	**3**
	(10 inch size)	

1. Put the cream cheese into the bowl. Use the fork to mash the cream cheese until smooth.

2. Add the icing sugar, pineapple and coconut. Mix well.

3. Divide the mixture among the tortillas. Spread with the knife. Roll each tortilla up like a jelly roll. Cover with plastic wrap. Chill for at least 1 hour. Cuts into 30, 1 inch pinwheels or 3 whole rolls.

Tip: Save the pineapple juice, chill and top up with some ginger ale and a cherry for a great beverage treat!

These will keep for several days in the fridge. Eat sliced or leave whole.

Seeded Cheese

GET READY ✔

measuring spoons, pie plate, oven mitts, wire rack, microwave-safe plate

1.	Sesame seeds	2 tbsp.
2.	Cheese (your favorite), cut into 10 sticks, ½ inch thick, ½ inch wide and about 3 inches long	6 oz.

1. Place the oven rack in the upper position (second from the top). Turn the oven on to broil. Place the sesame seeds in the ungreased pie plate. Broil the seeds in the oven for about 3 minutes, shaking the pie plate occasionally, using the oven mitts, until the seeds are golden brown. Use the oven mitts to remove the pie plate to the wire rack. Cool slightly.

2. Place the cheese on the microwave-safe plate. Microwave, uncovered, on high (100%) for 6 seconds until warm. Lightly press and roll the warmed cheese sticks in the seeds. Chill for 30 minutes. Makes about 10 cheese sticks.

Cheese lovers will devour these!

This is worth hurrying home from school to make. Recipe may be halved if desired. Do not freeze.

Nacho Two Step

GET READY ✓
cookie sheet, sharp knife, cutting board, paper towel, table spoon, medium bowl, dry measures, measuring spoons, mixing spoon, oven mitts, wire rack

1.	**Bag of tortilla chips**	**8 oz.**
2.	**Medium tomatoes**	**2**
	Can of diced green chilies, drained	**4 oz.**
	Sliced green onion	**¼ cup**
	Chili powder	**½ tsp.**
	Grated mild or medium Cheddar cheese	**¼ cup**
3.	**Grated Monterey Jack cheese**	**2 cups**

1. Place the rack in the center position in the oven. Turn the oven on to 350°F. Pour the tortilla chips onto the cookie sheet. Crowd them together so not much of the cookie sheet shows underneath.

2. Cut the tomatoes in half with the knife on the cutting board. Gently squeeze each half over the paper towel to remove the seeds. Use the table spoon to scoop out the rest. Throw away the seeds. Dice the tomato on the cutting board. Put into the bowl. Add the green chilies, green onion, chili powder and Cheddar cheese. Stir. Spoon over the chips.

3. Sprinkle the Monterey Jack cheese over the top. Bake in the oven for about 10 minutes until the cheese is melted. Use the oven mitts to remove the cookie sheet to the wire rack. Serves 2.

Left: Stuffed Pita, below; Right: Piece O'Pizza, page 29

Stuffed Pita

GET READY ✔
dry measures, measuring spoons, medium bowl, mixing spoon, table spoon, paper towel, microwave-safe plate

1.	Medium pita bread, cut in half	1
	Mozzarella cheese slices	4
2.	Cooked ham slices, slivered	2
	Small tomato, diced and drained	1
	Thinly sliced celery	¼ cup
	Seeded and grated cucumber, drained	½ cup
	Slivered red pepper	3 tbsp.
	Sweet pickle relish	2 tsp.
	Chopped iceberg lettuce	1 cup
	Salad dressing (or mayonnaise)	1 tbsp.
3.	Alfalfa sprouts (optional)	½ cup

1. Line each pita half with 2 slices of the cheese.

2. Mix the next 8 ingredients in the bowl. Spoon the mixture into the center of the pitas between the cheese slices. Arrange on the paper towel on the plate. Microwave on high (100%) for 1 to 2 minutes until the cheese melts.

3. Tuck the alfalfa sprouts around the top edges. Makes 2 servings.

Piece O'Pizza

GET READY ✔
dry measures, measuring spoons, 3 quart casserole dish, mixing spoon,
liquid measures, table knife, paper towel

1.	Lean ground beef	1 lb.
	Chopped onion	1 cup
	Medium green pepper, chopped	1
	Grated carrot	½ cup
	Salt	1½ tsp.
2.	Pizza sauce	1¼ cups
	Can of mushroom pieces, drained	10 oz.
3.	English muffins, split	3
	Pimiento-stuffed olives, sliced	18
	Grated medium Cheddar cheese	6 tbsp.
	Grated mozzarella cheese	6 tbsp.

1. Combine the first 5 ingredients in the casserole dish. Crumble together. Cover. Microwave on high (100%) for about 10 minutes, stirring at halftime, until no pink remains in the beef and vegetables are cooked.

2. Add the pizza sauce and mushrooms. Stir. Makes 5 cups.

3. Use the knife to spread 2 tbsp. beef mixture over each muffin half. Lay the slices of olives over each, followed by 1 tbsp. of each cheese. Arrange in a circle on the paper towel in the microwave. Microwave, uncovered, on high (100%) for about 55 seconds for each muffin half, rotating ½ turn at halftime if you don't have a turntable, until the cheese is melted. Allow 3 minutes for 6 muffin halves if done together. Freeze remaining beef mixture or make more pizzas. Makes 6 pizza muffins.

Pictured on page 28.

Vegetable Pizza

GET READY ✔
12 inch pizza pan, dry measures, liquid measures, small bowl, mixing spoon, oven mitts, wire rack, table knife, measuring spoons

1.	**Biscuit mix**	**1⅛ cups**
	Milk	**¼ cup**
2.	**Spaghetti sauce**	**¼ cup**
3.	**Grated mozzarella cheese**	**1 cup**
	Chopped green pepper	**2 tbsp.**
	Sliced fresh mushrooms	**¼ cup**
	Finely chopped onion	**2 tbsp.**
	Pitted ripe olives, sliced	**5-6**

1. Place the oven rack in the center position. Turn the oven on to 375°F. Grease the pizza pan. Mix the biscuit mix and milk in the bowl to make a soft dough. Press firmly on the pan with your hand. Bake in the oven for 15 minutes to partially cook. Use the oven mitts to remove the pizza pan to the wire rack.

2. Use the knife to spread the spaghetti sauce over the crust.

3. Sprinkle the cheese over the top. Sprinkle with the green pepper, mushrooms, onion and olives. Bake in the oven for about 15 minutes until the cheese has bubbled up through the toppings. Use the oven mitts to remove the pizza pan to the wire rack. Cuts into 6 wedges.

Make as cheesy as you like just by adding more or less cheese. You can also add more or less of your favorite toppings, too.

Made with English muffins, these are quick and easy to make. Sure to become a real hit.

Mock Pizza

GET READY ✔
baking sheet, measuring spoons, small bowl, mixing spoon, table knife, dry measures, oven mitts, wire rack

1.	English muffins, cut in half	6
2.	Can of tomato sauce	7½ oz.
	Dried sweet basil	¼ tsp.
	Ground oregano	¼ tsp.
	Onion powder	¼ tsp.
	Parsley flakes	¼ tsp.
	Seasoned salt	½ tsp.
3.	Grated mozzarella cheese	1 cup
	Cherry tomatoes, sliced	12
	Small fresh mushrooms, sliced	12
	Bite-size pepperoni pieces	60
4.	Grated mozzarella cheese	⅓ cup

1. Place the oven rack in the top position. Turn the oven on to broil. Arrange the muffin halves on the ungreased baking sheet.

2. Stir the next 6 ingredients in the bowl. Divide and spread the mixture over the muffin halves with the knife.

3. Layer the next 4 ingredients over the tomato sauce in the order given.

4. Sprinkle the second amount of cheese over the pepperoni. Heat under the broiler until the cheese is melted and bubbly. Use the oven mitts to remove the baking sheet to the wire rack. Serves 4.

Tomato Mozza Rounds

GET READY ✔

measuring spoons, small bowl, mixing spoon, baking sheet, oven mitts, wire rack, pancake lifter, table spoon, dry measures

1. Medium tomato, chopped   1
   Olive oil   1 tbsp.
   Garlic powder   ⅛ tsp.
   Salt   ¼ tsp.
   Grated Parmesan cheese   2 tsp.
   Dried sweet basil   1 tsp.

2. French bread slices (cut 1 inch thick)   2

3. Grated mozzarella cheese   ¼ cup
   Pitted ripe olives, sliced (optional)

A kid's type bruschetta (pronounced broo-SKET-ah).

1. Place the rack in the oven in the top position. Turn the oven on to broil. Combine the first 6 ingredients in the bowl. Mix well.

2. Place the bread slices on the ungreased baking sheet. Heat under the broiler until browned. Use the oven mitts to remove the baking sheet to the wire rack to cool slightly. Turn the bread over with the pancake lifter. Spoon the tomato mixture on the untoasted side of the bread.

3. Sprinkle with the cheese and olives. Heat under the broiler until the cheese is melted. Use the oven mitts to remove the baking sheet to the wire rack. Let stand for 1 minute. Makes 2 large rounds.

Cracker Nachos

GET READY ✔
9 × 9 inch square baking pan, dry measures, measuring spoons, oven mitts, wire rack, table spoon

1.	**Triscuit crackers**	**20**
2.	**Grated Cheddar cheese**	**½ cup**
	Green onions, sliced	**2**
	Medium green pepper, finely chopped	**½**
	Imitation bacon bits (or crisp cooked bacon, crumbled)	**2 tbsp.**
	Grated Cheddar cheese	**½ cup**
3.	**Salsa (optional)**	

1. Place the oven rack in the center position. Turn the oven on to 350°F. Place the crackers close together in the ungreased pan.

2. Sprinkle the first amount of cheese, green onion, green pepper and bacon bits over top of the crackers. Sprinkle with the second amount of cheese. Bake, uncovered, in the oven for 15 minutes. Use the oven mitts to remove the pan to the wire rack.

3. Spoon the salsa on top. Serves 4.

A very easy whole wheat version of nachos.

Pita Pizzas

GET READY ✔

measuring spoons, table knife, dry measures, baking sheet, oven mitts, wire rack

1. Pita breads 2
   Pizza sauce .... 3 tbsp.

2. Any combination to make .... ⅔ cup
   (chopped fresh mushrooms,
   chopped green pepper, chopped
   tomato, chopped green onion,
   pineapple tidbits, cooked
   crumbled bacon, deli meat such
   as ham or pepperoni)

3. Grated mozzarella cheese .... ½ cup

1. Place the oven rack in the center position. Turn the oven on to broil. Spread each pita with 1½ tbsp. sauce with the knife, spreading to the edges.

2. Sprinkle 1 pita with ½ of the toppings. Repeat.

3. Sprinkle the cheese over the toppings. Lay the pitas on the ungreased baking sheet. Heat under the broiler for 8 to 9 minutes until the cheese is melted and the edges are crispy. Use the oven mitts to remove the baking sheet to the wire rack. Makes 2 pita pizzas.

These pizzas can be assembled and frozen before baking. When those hunger pangs hit, pop the frozen pizza in the oven and broil for eight to nine minutes.

The chunkier the salsa, the better! Serve with a dollop of sour cream.

Quesadillas

GET READY ✔

baking sheet, dry measures, table knife, pancake lifter, oven mitts, wire rack

1.	**White (or whole wheat) flour tortilla (10 inch size)**	**1**
2.	**Chunky salsa**	**⅓ cup**
	Grated Cheddar cheese	**⅓ cup**

1. Place the oven rack in the center position. Turn the oven on to 400°F. Lay the tortilla out flat on the ungreased baking sheet.

2. Use the knife to spread the salsa on ½ of the tortilla. Sprinkle with the cheese. Fold the other ½ of the tortilla over top of the cheese. Press down lightly with your hand. Bake in the oven for 4 minutes. Use the pancake lifter to turn the quesadilla over. Bake for 4 minutes. Use the oven mitts to remove the baking sheet to the wire rack. Cool slightly. Cuts into 3 wedges.

This tuna sandwich is warmed in the oven and makes a nice warm treat on a chilly day.

Toasty Tuna Torpedoes

GET READY ✔
dry measures, measuring spoons, medium bowl, mixing spoon, sharp knife, cutting board, 4 large pieces of foil, oven mitts, 4 small plates

1.	Can of tuna, drained and flaked	6½ oz.
	Grated Cheddar cheese	1 cup
	Chopped dill pickle	2 tbsp.
	Green onion, thinly sliced	1
2.	Prepared mustard	1 tbsp.
	Salad dressing (or mayonnaise)	1 tbsp.
3.	Hot dog buns	4

1. Place the oven rack in the center position. Turn the oven on to 350°F. Combine the tuna, cheese, pickle and green onion in the bowl. Stir.

2. Add the mustard and salad dressing. Stir.

3. Cut the hot dog buns horizontally with the knife on the cutting board, making sure to not cut all the way through. Open the buns and stuff with the tuna mixture. Wrap in the foil. Bake in the oven for 15 minutes. Use the oven mitts to remove the sandwiches to the plates. Cool each sandwich slightly before unwrapping. Makes 4 torpedoes.

Bean Quesadillas

1.	White (or whole wheat) flour tortilla (10 inch size)	1
2.	Refried beans with green chilies	⅓ cup
3.	Small tomato	1
	Grated Cheddar cheese	½ cup

1. Place the oven rack in the center position. Turn the oven on to 400°F. Lay the tortilla out flat on the ungreased baking sheet.

2. Spread the beans over the tortilla with the table knife.

3. Cut the tomato in half with the sharp knife on the cutting board. Gently squeeze over the paper towel to remove the seeds. Use the table spoon to scoop out the rest. Throw away the seeds and juice. Dice the tomato into small chunks on the cutting board. Sprinkle the tomato and cheese over ½ of the beans. Fold the plain bean half over the bean, tomato and cheese half. Press down lightly with your hand. Bake in the oven for 10 minutes. Use the oven mitts to remove the baking sheet to the wire rack. Let stand for 3 to 5 minutes before cutting. Cuts into 6 wedges.

Macaroni Magic

GET READY ✔

large saucepan, dry measures, mixing spoon, 8 inch casserole dish, sharp knife, cutting board, paper towel, table spoon, small bowl, measuring spoons, oven mitts, wire rack

1.	**Package of macaroni and cheese dinner**	**6½ oz.**
	Chopped onion	**¾ cup**
2.	**Can of sliced mushrooms, drained**	**10 oz.**
	Can of flaked chicken	**6½ oz.**
3.	**Large tomato**	**1**
	Dried sweet basil	**1 tsp.**
	Granulated sugar	**¼ tsp.**
	Salt, light sprinkle	
	Pepper, light sprinkle	

1. Place the oven rack in the center position. Turn the oven on to 350°F. Prepare the macaroni and cheese in the saucepan as the package directs, adding the onion before cooking.

2. Stir the mushrooms and chicken into the prepared macaroni. Turn into the casserole dish.

3. Cut the tomato in half with the knife on the cutting board. Gently squeeze over the paper towel to remove the seeds. Use the table spoon to scoop out the rest. Throw away the seeds and juice. Chop the tomato on the cutting board. Put into the bowl. Add the basil and sugar. Stir. Sprinkle with the salt and pepper. Stir. Pile on the center of the casserole. Cover. Bake in the oven for 20 to 30 minutes until heated through. Use the oven mitts to remove the casserole dish to the wire rack. Serves 4.

Pictured on page 39.

Bologna Cups, below, make a wonderful container to fill with Macaroni Magic, page 38.

Bologna Cups

GET READY ✔

frying pan, table fork

1. Bologna slices   **4**

1. Fry the bologna in the frying pan for about 2 minutes. They will puff up in the center. Do not flatten. Turn the slices over with the fork. Fry for about 1 minute. Turn the "cups" right side up. Makes 4.

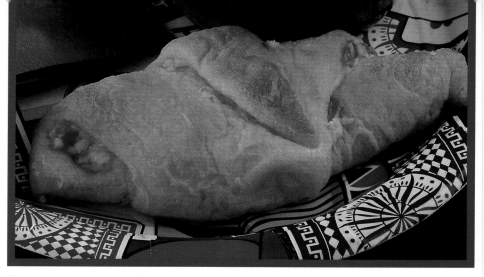

These are great warm or cold.

Ham & Cheese Delights

GET READY ✔
measuring spoons, medium bowl, mixing spoon, table knife, baking sheet, oven mitts, wire rack

1.	**Cream cheese, softened**	**8 oz.**
	Sweet pickle relish	**1½ tbsp**
	Ham slices, diced	**5**
	Onion powder	**¼ tsp.**
2.	**Refrigerator crescent-style rolls (tube of 8)**	**8½ oz.**

1. Place the oven rack in the center position. Turn the oven on to 375°F. Combine the cream cheese, relish, ham and onion powder in the bowl. Mix well.

2. Open the crescent roll tube and separate the rolls into 8 triangles. Use the knife to spread 2 tbsp. ham mixture on each triangle. Roll from the shortest side of the triangle to the opposite point. Place the rolls on the ungreased baking sheet. Bake in the oven for 12 minutes until golden brown. Use the oven mitts to remove the baking sheet to the wire rack. Makes 8 "delights."

Corn Doggies

GET READY ✔
medium bowl, dry measures, measuring spoons, mixing spoon, table fork, rolling pin, ruler, table knife, baking sheet, pastry brush, oven mitts, wire rack

1. | | |
   |---|---|
   | Envelope of pie crust mix (9½ oz.) | 1 |
   | Yellow cornmeal | ⅓ cup |
   | Chili powder | 1 tsp. |
   | Cold water, approximately | 6 tbsp. |
   | All-purpose flour, as needed, to prevent sticking when rolling | |

2. | | |
   |---|---|
   | Wieners | 8 |
   | Large egg, fork-beaten | 1 |

1. Place the oven rack in the center position. Turn the oven on to 450°F. Pour the pie crust mix into the bowl. Stir in the cornmeal and chili powder. Slowly add the cold water, 1 tbsp. at a time, stirring with the fork after each addition. The dough should start to pull away from the sides of the bowl and form a ball. Divide in half. Roll each half into a 5 × 12 inch rectangle on a lightly floured counter or working surface. Cut each rectangle crosswise into 4 equal rectangles.

2. Place a wiener lengthwise across each rectangle. Brush the egg on 1 of the long edges of the pastry. Bring the 2 long edges of the rectangle up over the wiener and press together to seal. Place, seam-side down, on the ungreased baking sheet. Repeat with each rectangle. Brush the remaining egg on each surface. Bake in the oven for 12 minutes until crisp and golden brown. Use the oven mitts to remove the baking sheet to the wire rack. Makes 8 wrapped wieners.

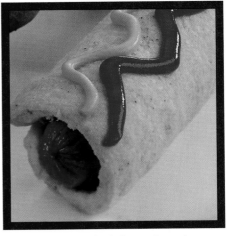

Make these the night before and simply reheat when you get home from school. These also freeze well.

Pizza Sticks

GET READY ✔
baking sheet, dry measures, measuring spoons, large bowl, mixing spoon, liquid measures, rolling pin, ruler, sharp knife, cutting board, tea towel, small cup, pastry brush, oven mitts, wire rack

1.		
All-purpose flour	2 cups
Salt	½ tsp.
Granulated sugar	¼ tsp.
Dried sweet basil	½ tsp.
Instant yeast	1 tbsp.
Olive (or cooking) oil	1½ tbsp.
Hot water	1 cup
All-purpose flour, approximately	½ cup
Chopped pepperoni	⅔ cup
2.		
Hard margarine, melted	2 tbsp.
Garlic powder	¼ tsp.

1. Place the oven rack in the center position. Grease the baking sheet. Stir the first 5 ingredients together in the bowl. Pour in the olive oil and hot water. Stir until the flour is combined. Work in the second amount of flour until the dough is no longer sticky. Turn out onto a lightly floured surface. Knead for about 5 minutes, adding more flour as needed and a bit of the chopped pepperoni, until all the pepperoni is mixed into the dough. Invert the bowl over the dough. Let the dough rest for 10 minutes. Roll the dough out to about ½ inch thick. Cut rows about 1 inch wide with the knife on the cutting board. Cut crosswise into 5 inch sticks. Lay each stick on the baking sheet, about 2 inches apart. Cover with the tea towel. Let rise in the oven, with the door closed and the oven light on, for 30 minutes.

2. Remove the baking sheet from the oven. Turn the oven on to 375°F. Combine the melted margarine and garlic powder in the cup. Brush the sticks with the margarine mixture. Bake in the oven for 20 minutes. Use the oven mitts to remove the baking sheet to the wire rack. Makes 18 to 20 sticks.

Slightly crusty golden strips of bread.
Specks of pepperoni throughout. Nippy taste.

Kid Kabobs

GET READY ✔

4 inch wooden bamboo skewer, small microwave-safe plate

1. **Wiener cubes (1 wiener)**   **3**
   Gherkin   **1**
   Pineapple chunk (from can)   **1**

1. Thread the wooden skewer with 1 wiener cube, the pickle, another wiener cube, the pineapple chunk and the last wiener cube. Lay on the plate. Microwave, uncovered, on high (100%) for about 30 seconds until hot. Makes 1 kabob.

Frankfurter Flower

GET READY ✔

sharp knife, cutting board, small microwave-safe plate, wooden toothpicks

1. **Wieners**   **2**

2. **Ketchup, for dipping**
   Prepared mustard, for dipping

1. Cut 1 wiener in half crosswise with the knife on the cutting board. Place the halves side by side on the small plate. Run the 2 wooden toothpicks through them so they will stay flat. Cut the second wiener into ½ inch pieces. Pierce each small piece of the wiener with the wooden toothpick. Place the other end of the toothpick in the wiener base. Set on the plate. Microwave, uncovered, on high (100%) for 50 to 60 seconds until hot.

2. Dip into the ketchup and mustard. When the small pieces are eaten, cut up the 2 larger bottom wieners and pierce with the toothpicks. Makes 1.

Top Center: Frankfurter Flower, above
Right: Kid Kabobs, this page
Bottom: Pita Bean Snack, page 45

Sneaky Snack

GET READY ✔
sharp knife, cutting board, shallow microwave-safe bowl, measuring spoons, mixing spoon, oven mitts, hot pad

1.	**Wieners**	**2**
2.	**Grape (or apple or red currant) jelly**	**1 tbsp.**
	Chili sauce (or ketchup)	**1 tbsp.**

1. Cut each wiener into 6 or 7 pieces with the knife on the cutting board. Place all the pieces in the bowl.

2. Spoon the jelly and chili sauce over the wiener slices. Stir to coat. Microwave on high (100%) for 2 minutes. Stir. Use the oven mitts to remove the bowl to the hot pad. Serves 2.

You can't get any easier than this. Have paper napkins and wooden toothpicks handy.

Pita Bean Snack

GET READY ✔
1 quart casserole dish, mixing spoon, sharp knife, cutting board, table spoon

1.	**Can of pork and beans**	**14 oz.**
	Wieners, thinly sliced	**2**
2.	**Small pita breads**	**4**

1. Combine the pork and beans and wieners in the casserole dish. Stir. Cover. Microwave on high (100%) for about 2 1/2 minutes until hot.

2. Cut open the tops of the pitas with the knife on the cutting board. Spoon about 1/4 cup meat mixture into each. Makes 4.

Pictured on page 44.

French Fries

GET READY ✔

baking sheet, table fork, oven mitts, wire rack

1.	Medium potatoes, peeled and cut into sticks or slices	6
	Salt, sprinkle	
	Pepper, sprinkle	

1. Place the oven rack in the center position. Turn the oven on to 425°F. Grease the baking sheet. Spread the potato pieces in a single layer on the baking sheet. Bake in the oven for about 5 minutes until the centers are fairly tender when pierced with the fork. Use the oven mitts to remove the baking sheet to the wire rack. Sprinkle with the salt and pepper. Serves 6.

Kids of all ages will dive into these. These can be frozen in a single layer for 1 hour then transferred to a plastic freezer bag. To prepare, spread on a greased baking sheet and bake in a 425°F oven for about 5 minutes.

Make this sandwich when you want to try a really different tasting grilled cheese sandwich.

Pineapple Grilled Cheese

GET READY ✔
frying pan, measuring spoons, small cup, mixing spoon, table knife, pancake lifter, medium plate

1.	**Canned crushed pineapple, well drained**	**2 tbsp.**
	Finely chopped pecans (optional)	**2 tsp.**
2.	**Yellow cheese slices**	**2**
	White (or whole wheat) bread slices, buttered on 1 side	**2**

1. Heat the frying pan on medium-low. Combine the pineapple and pecans in the cup. Stir.

2. Put 1 cheese slice on the unbuttered side of a slice of bread. Use the knife to spread the pineapple mixture on top of the cheese. Lay the second cheese slice over the pineapple. Lay the second bread slice, butter-side up, on top of the cheese. Place the sandwich in the frying pan. When the bottom side is browned, use the pancake lifter to flip the sandwich over to brown the other side. Use the lifter to remove the sandwich to the plate. Makes 1 sandwich.

Snuggly Dogs

GET READY ✔

baking sheet, dry measures, measuring spoons, medium bowl, mixing spoon, pastry blender, liquid measures, table fork, rolling pin, sharp knife, cutting board, oven mitts, wire rack

1.	All-purpose flour	2 cups
	Baking powder	4 tsp.
	Granulated sugar	2 tbsp.
	Salt	1 tsp.
	Hard margarine	⅓ cup
2.	Milk	¾ cup
3.	Wieners, heated and wiped dry	12

1. Place the oven rack in the center position. Turn the oven on to 425°F. Grease the baking sheet. Mix the first 4 ingredients in the bowl. Use the pastry blender to cut in the margarine until crumbly.

2. Add the milk. Stir with the fork until the dough forms a ball. Add a bit more milk, if necessary, to make a soft dough. Turn out onto a lightly floured surface. Knead 10 times. Roll the dough ¼ inch thick with the rolling pin. Cut into 12 rectangles with the knife on the cutting board.

3. Completely enclose each wiener in 1 portion of the dough. Dampen the edges of the dough. Press together to seal. Arrange on the baking sheet. Bake in the oven for 8 to 10 minutes until risen and golden brown. Use the oven mitts to remove the baking sheet to the wire rack. Makes 12 dogs.

Fun biscuits to fill hungry tummies.

Chewy Peanut Bars

GET READY ✔
9 × 13 inch oblong baking pan, dry measures, large saucepan, long-handled mixing spoon, hot pad

1.	Creamed honey	¾ cup
	Smooth peanut butter	1 cup
2.	Semisweet chocolate chips	1 cup
	Large white marshmallows	10
3.	Crisp rice cereal	3 cups
	Salted peanuts, finely chopped	1 cup

1. Grease the pan. Set aside. Combine the honey and peanut butter in the saucepan. Heat on low, stirring occasionally, until just boiling. Remove the saucepan to the hot pad.

2. Add the chocolate chips and marshmallows. Stir until melted.

3. Add the cereal and peanuts. Grease your hands slightly. Pack the peanut mixture into the pan, pressing firmly and evenly. Chill. Cuts into 18 bars.

These are just like a popular chocolate bar.

Top Left: Chocolate Crisps, page 51, Top Right: Puffed Wheat Squares, page 51,
Bottom Right: Chocolate Confetti, below

Chocolate Confetti

GET READY ✔
9 x 9 inch square baking pan, dry measures, large saucepan, long-handled mixing spoon, hot pad

1.	**Hard margarine**	**¼ cup**
	Smooth peanut butter	**½ cup**
	Semisweet chocolate chips	**1 cup**
2.	**Miniature colored marshmallows**	**8 oz.**

1. Grease the pan. Set aside. Melt the margarine and peanut butter in the saucepan. Stir in the chocolate chips until melted. Remove the saucepan to the hot pad. Cool so that you can hold your hand on the bottom of the saucepan.

2. Add the marshmallows. Stir until well coated. Press firmly in the pan with your hand. Chill. Cuts into 36 squares.

Variation: To the above ingredients add ½ cup chopped walnuts and/or ½ cup medium coconut.

50 Squares

Puffed Wheat Squares

GET READY ✔

8 × 8 inch square baking pan, dry measures, liquid measures, measuring spoons, small saucepan, long-handled mixing spoon, hot pad, large bowl

1.	Hard margarine	¼ cup
	Light or dark corn syrup	⅓ cup
	Brown sugar, packed	½ cup
	Cocoa powder	1½ tbsp.
2.	Puffed wheat cereal	6 cups

1. Grease the pan. Set aside. Combine the margarine, corn syrup, brown sugar and cocoa powder in the saucepan. Heat on medium, stirring constantly, until the mixture begins to bubble. Boil for 1½ minutes. Remove the saucepan to the hot pad.

2. Pour the mixture over the cereal in the bowl. Stir until all of the cereal is coated. Press firmly in the pan with your hand. Chill for 15 minutes before cutting. Cuts into 25 squares.

Pictured on page 50.

Chocolate Crisps

GET READY ✔

9 × 9 inch square baking pan, liquid measures, dry measures, large saucepan, long-handled mixing spoon, hot pad

1.	Liquid honey	¾ cup
	Smooth peanut butter	1 cup
2.	Semisweet chocolate chips	1 cup
3.	Salted peanuts	1 cup
	Crisp rice cereal	3 cups

1. Grease the pan. Set aside. Melt the honey and peanut butter in the saucepan on low, stirring occasionally. Bring the mixture to a boil. Remove the saucepan to the hot pad.

2. Add the chocolate chips. Stir until melted.

3. Add the peanuts and cereal. Stir to coat. Press firmly in the pan with your hand. Chill well before cutting. Cuts into 36 squares.

Pictured on page 50.

Puffed Wheat Cake

GET READY ✔
large bowl, 9 × 9 inch square baking pan, dry measures, measuring spoons, large
heavy saucepan, long-handled mixing spoon, candy thermometer, table spoon,
hot pad

1.	Brown sugar, packed	1 cup
	Creamed honey	½ cup
	Hard margarine	½ cup
	Cocoa powder	2 tbsp.
2.	Vanilla flavoring	½ tsp.
3.	Puffed wheat cereal	6 cups
	Crisp rice cereal	2 cups

1. Grease the bowl and pan. Set aside. Combine the first 4 ingredients in the saucepan. Heat on medium-high, stirring often, until the mixture boils. Boil for 5 to 8 minutes until the temperature reaches the soft ball stage (about 235°F on the candy thermometer) or until a small spoonful forms a soft ball in cold water.

2. Remove the saucepan from the heat to the hot pad. Stir in the vanilla flavoring.

3. Combine both of the cereals in the bowl. Pour the hot honey mixture over the cereals. Stir to coat well. Press firmly in the pan with your hand. Let stand until cool and set. Cuts into 36 pieces.

Top: Puffed Wheat Cake, above
Bottom: Brownie Cupcakes, page 53

Brownie Cupcakes

GET READY ✔
dry measures, medium saucepan, long-handled mixing spoon, hot pad, measuring spoons, muffin pan (enough for 12 muffins), wooden toothpick, oven mitts, wire rack, small bowl, mixing spoon

1.	Semisweet chocolate baking squares (1 oz. each), chopped	2
	Hard margarine	½ cup
2.	Brown sugar, packed	1½ cups
	All-purpose flour	1 cup
	Large eggs, fork-beaten	2
	Vanilla flavoring	1 tsp.
	Chopped pecans (or walnuts)	½ cup
	Salt	¼ tsp.
3.	**CHOCOLATE ICING**	
	Hard margarine, softened	3 tbsp.
	Icing (confectioner's) sugar	1½ cups
	Cocoa powder	⅓ cup
	Water (or milk or coffee)	2 tbsp.

1. Place the oven rack in the center position. Turn the oven on to 350°F. Melt the chocolate and margarine in the saucepan on low, stirring often. Remove the saucepan to the hot pad.

2. Add the remaining 6 ingredients. Stir just enough to moisten. Grease the muffin pan. Spoon into the muffin pan, filling ½ full. Bake in the oven for 20 to 25 minutes until the wooden toothpick inserted in the center comes out clean. Use the oven mitts to remove the muffine pan to the wire rack. Cool.

3. **Chocolate Icing:** Mix the margarine, icing sugar and cocoa powder in the small bowl. Add just enough of the water to make a barely pourable consistency. Spread on cooled cupcakes. Makes 12.

Pictured on page 52.

Jellied Marshmallows

GET READY ✔

8 × 8 inch square baking pan, waxed paper, liquid measures, small saucepan, long-handled mixing spoon, dry measures, measuring spoons, medium bowl, rubber spatula, electric mixer, small sieve, damp tea towel, sharp knife

1. Package of any flavor gelatin (jelly powder)   **3 oz.**
    Boiling water   **⅔ cup**
    Granulated sugar   **1 cup**
    White corn syrup   **3 tbsp.**

2. Icing (confectioner's) sugar, for coating

Top: Midnight Mints, page 55
Bottom: Jellied Marshmallows,
this page

1. Line the pan with the waxed paper. Combine the jelly powder and boiling water in the saucepan. Heat on low, stirring constantly, until dissolved. Add the granulated sugar, stirring constantly, until dissolved. Stir in the corn syrup. Turn into the bowl. Cool. Place the rubber spatula in the bowl. Chill for 10 minutes. Stir, scraping down sides of the bowl. Chill for 10 minute intervals, stirring and scraping sides down, until the mixture is almost as stiff as liquid honey, but not chunky. Beat on high with the mixer for 5 minutes until stiff. Pour into the waxed paper-lined pan. Chill overnight.

2. Use the sieve to sift some of the icing sugar onto the countertop or breadboard at least the size of the pan. Turn out the entire jellied square onto the icing sugar. Gently rub the damp tea towel over the waxed paper. Let stand for a few minutes. Pull off the waxed paper. Dust the top of the square with the icing sugar. Cut into squares with the knife, dusting each new cut surface with the icing sugar. Cuts into 25 squares.

54 Squares

Midnight Mints

GET READY ✔
dry measures, large saucepan, long-handled mixing spoon, measuring spoons, liquid measures, hot pad, 9 x 9 inch square baking pan, small bowl, table knife, small saucepan

1. BOTTOM LAYER	
Hard margarine	½ cup
Granulated sugar	¼ cup
Cocoa powder	⅓ cup
Large egg, fork-beaten	1
2. Graham cracker crumbs	1¾ cups
Finely chopped walnuts	½ cup
Fine coconut	¾ cup
3. SECOND LAYER	
Hard margarine, softened	⅓ cup
Milk	3 tbsp.
Peppermint flavoring	1 tsp.
Icing (confectioner's) sugar	2 cups
Drops of green food coloring	2-3
4. TOP LAYER	
Semisweet chocolate chips	⅔ cup
Hard margarine	2 tbsp.

1. **Bottom Layer:** Combine the margarine, sugar and cocoa powder in the large saucepan on medium. Stir. Heat until the mixture boils. Remove 3 tbsp. mixture to the liquid measure. Add the egg slowly, stirring constantly. Add the egg mixture to the saucepan slowly, stirring constantly, until thickened. Remove the saucepan to the hot pad.

2. Stir in the graham crumbs, walnuts and coconut. Mix well. Grease the pan. Pack the crumb mixture very firmly in the pan.

3. **Second Layer:** Combine the margarine, milk, peppermint flavoring and icing sugar in the bowl. Beat together well. Add a bit more of the milk if needed to make the mixture spreadable. Tint green with the food coloring. Spread over the first layer with the knife.

4. **Top Layer:** Melt the chocolate chips and margarine in the small saucepan on low, stirring often. Cool. When cool but still runny, spread over the second layer. Chill. Cuts into 36 squares.

Pictured on page 54.

Chocolate Oh Henry Squares

GET READY ✔
9 x 9 inch square baking pan, sharp knife, dry measures, liquid measures, large saucepan, long-handled mixing spoon, hot pad, measuring spoons, small bowl, electric mixer, rubber spatula

1.	Whole graham crackers	14
2.	Hard margarine	¾ cup
	Brown sugar, packed	⅔ cup
	Milk	½ cup
3.	Semisweet chocolate chips	⅓ cup
	Graham cracker crumbs	1¼ cups
	Chopped walnuts	1 cup
4.	Whole graham crackers	14
5.	**ICING**	
	Icing (confectioner's) sugar	1¼ cups
	Hard margarine, softened	3 tbsp.
	Cocoa powder	¼ cup
	Hot prepared coffee	1½ tbsp.

1. Line the ungreased pan with the first amount of graham crackers, trimming to fit with the knife.

2. Combine the margarine, brown sugar and milk in the saucepan. Stir. Heat on medium until the mixture comes to a boil.

3. Remove the saucepan to the hot pad. Add the chocolate chips. Stir to melt. Add the graham crumbs and walnuts. Mix. Pour over the crackers in the pan.

4. Cover with the second amount of whole graham crackers, trimming to fit. Cool.

5. **Icing:** Beat the icing sugar, margarine, cocoa powder and coffee in the bowl with the mixer, adding more liquid or icing sugar as needed for spreading consistency. Spread over the squares with the rubber spatula. Cover. Let stand for a few hours to soften the crackers before cutting. Cuts into 36 squares.

Pictured on page 57.

Rice Crispies

GET READY ✔
8 × 8 inch square baking pan, dry measures, large saucepan,
long-handled mixing spoon

1.	**Hard margarine**	**¼ cup**
2.	**Large white marshmallows**	**32**
3.	**Crisp rice cereal**	**5 cups**

1. Grease the pan. Set aside. Melt the margarine in the saucepan.

2. Add the marshmallows. Stir on low until melted.

3. Add the cereal. Stir to coat well. Press firmly in the pan with your hand. Let
    stand for a few hours to set before cutting. Cuts into 25 squares.

Variation: Melt 3 tbsp. hard margarine and 1 cup semisweet chocolate chips on low,
stirring often. Spread over the top.

Left: Rice Crispies, above
Right: Chocolate Oh Henry
Squares, page 56

Creamy Jelly Jiggles

GET READY ✔
9 x 13 inch oblong baking pan, medium bowl, mixing spoon, liquid measures, sharp knife (or cookie cutters)

1.	Envelopes of unflavored gelatin (equivalent to 1 tbsp. each)	2
	Packages of lime-flavored gelatin (jelly powder), 3 oz. each	2
2.	Boiling water	1⅔ cups
3.	Half-and-half (light cream)	⅔ cup

1. Lightly grease the pan. Set aside. Pour both the unflavored and flavored gelatins into the bowl. Mix well.

2. Add the boiling water to the gelatin in the bowl. Stir until the gelatins dissolve.

3. Add the half-and-half. Stir. Pour into the pan. Chill for at least 3 hours. Cut into squares with the knife or into your favorite shapes with the cookie cutters.

These jiggles settle into layers for a different look. Do not freeze.

Jelly Jiggles

GET READY ✔
9 × 13 inch oblong baking pan, medium bowl, mixing spoon, liquid measures, sharp knife (or cookie cutters)

1. **Envelopes of unflavored gelatin**   2
     (equivalent to 1 tbsp. each)
    Envelopes of orange-flavored gelatin   2
     (jelly powder), 3 oz. each

2. **Boiling water**   2½ cups

1. Lightly grease the pan. Set aside. Pour both the unflavored and flavored gelatins into the bowl. Mix well.

2. Add the boiling water to the bowl. Stir until the gelatins are dissolved. Pour into the pan. Chill for at least 3 hours until set. Cut into squares with the knife or into your favorite shapes with the cookie cutters.

Great to have ready in the refrigerator! Do not freeze.

Sweet Treats **59**

One is not enough!

Juice Jigglies

GET READY ✓
9 × 9 inch square baking pan, liquid measures, medium saucepan, long-handled
mixing spoon, hot pad, sharp knife (or cookie cutters)

1. **Cold water**	1½ cups
Envelopes of unflavored gelatin	4
(equivalent to 1 tbsp. each)	
2. **Frozen concentrated grape juice**	12 oz.
(or cranberry or raspberry cocktail),	
see Note	

1. Grease the pan. Set aside. Put the water into the saucepan. Sprinkle the gelatin over the top. Let stand for 1 minute. Heat on medium, stirring frequently, until the mixture comes to a boil. Remove the saucepan to the hot pad.

2. Add the juice concentrate. Stir until dissolved. Pour the mixture into the pan. Chill for 1 to 2 hours until set. Cut into squares with the knife or into your favorite shapes with the cookie cutters.

Note: Do not use a citrus concentrate such as orange, lemon or pineapple.

Apple Lime Freezies

GET READY ✔
liquid measures, medium saucepan, hot pad, long-handled mixing spoon, dry measures, 10 plastic drink cups (5 oz. size), foil, 10 wooden popsicle sticks (available at craft stores)

1.	Apple juice	2 cups
2.	Package of lime-flavored gelatin (jelly powder)	3 oz.
3.	Apple juice	2 cups
	Applesauce	1 cup

1. Pour the first amount of apple juice into the saucepan. Heat on medium-high until just starting to boil.

2. Remove the saucepan to the hot pad. Add the lime gelatin. Stir until dissolved.

3. Add the second amount of apple juice and applesauce. Stir. Pour the mixture into the drink cups to ¾ full. Place a piece of foil over each cup. Cut a small slit in the middle. Fit the popsicle sticks in through the foil. Freeze. To remove the popsicle, run hot water on the bottom of the cup until the popsicle slides out. Makes 10 popsicles.

The color is great! And the lime taste is refreshing.

A chewy cookie. Store the cookies in a covered container with waxed paper between the layers.

Chocolate Oat Chippers

GET READY ✔
dry measures, measuring spoons, large bowl, electric mixer, mixing spoon, cookie sheet, oven mitts, wire rack, pancake lifter, waxed paper

1.	Hard margarine, softened	½ cup
	Brown sugar, packed	1 cup
	Large egg	1
	Vanilla flavoring	½ tsp.
2.	All-purpose flour	1 cup
	Quick rolled oats (not instant)	1 cup
	Baking soda	½ tsp.
	Salt	¼ tsp.
	Semisweet chocolate chips	1 cup
	Chopped walnuts (optional)	½ cup

1. Place the oven rack in the center position. Turn the oven on to 350°F. Put the margarine, brown sugar, egg and vanilla flavoring into the bowl. Beat with the mixer on medium speed until smooth.

2. Add the remaining 6 ingredients. Stir with the spoon until all of the flour is mixed in. Grease the cookie sheet. Drop by rounded tablespoonfuls, 2 inches apart, onto the cookie sheet. This will allow room for the cookies to spread out. Bake in the oven for 10 to 12 minutes. Use the oven mitts to remove the cookie sheet to the wire rack. Let stand for 2 minutes. Use the pancake lifter to remove the cookies to the waxed paper on the counter. Cool completely. Makes about 3 dozen cookies.

Chocolate Bar Cookies

GET READY ✔
dry measures, medium bowl, mixing spoon, measuring spoons, rubber spatula, thick plastic bag, rolling pin, cookie sheet, oven mitts, wire rack, pancake lifter, waxed paper

1.	**Hard margarine, softened**	**½ cup**
	Brown sugar, packed	**⅓ cup**
	Granulated sugar	**⅓ cup**
2.	**Vanilla flavoring**	**1 tsp.**
	Large egg, fork-beaten	**1**
3.	**All-purpose flour**	**1¼ cups**
	Baking soda	**½ tsp.**
	Salt	**¼ tsp.**
4.	**Butter crunch chocolate bars (1½ oz. each)**	**2**

1. Place the oven rack in the center position. Turn the oven on to 375°F. Cream the margarine and both sugars together in the bowl until smooth.

2. Stir in the vanilla flavoring and egg.

3. Add the flour, baking soda and salt. Mix well, scraping down the sides of the bowl with the spatula.

4. Place the chocolate bars in the plastic bag. Break the bars into chunky pieces by hitting them with the rolling pin. Stir the chunks into the dough. Drop by rounded tablespoonfuls, about 2 inches apart, onto the ungreased cookie sheet. Bake in the oven for 10 minutes until the edges are browned. Centers will stay soft. Use the oven mitts to remove the cookie sheet to the wire rack. Let stand for 1 minute. Use the pancake lifter to remove the cookies to the waxed paper to cool completely. Makes 24 cookies.

Dotted with chocolate. Soft and chewy.
Just right with a glass of milk.

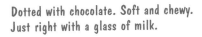

Let an adult show you how to core the apple the first time you make this. For a chewy texture, use Crumble Topping, page 21, to fill the cavity instead of the brown sugar and cinnamon.

Microwave Baked Apple

GET READY ✔
vegetable peeler, small microwave-safe bowl, measuring spoons, small cup, small table spoon

1.	**Medium cooking apple (such as McIntosh)**	**1**
2.	**Brown sugar, packed**	**1 tbsp.**
	Ground cinnamon	**⅛ tsp.**
3.	**Margarine**	**1 tsp.**

1. Wash the apple well. Remove the stem. Pierce down into the middle of the apple several times with the vegetable peeler, digging out as much of the core as possible. Put the apple into the bowl.

2. Combine the brown sugar and cinnamon in the cup. Stir. Sprinkle into the middle of the apple.

3. Top the apple with the margarine. Microwave on high (100%) for 2 minutes until the apple is tender. Cool slightly. Makes 1 apple.

Baked Apples

GET READY ✔
vegetable peeler, 1 quart casserole dish, measuring spoons, small cup

1.	**Medium cooking apples (such as McIntosh)**	**2**
2.	**Raisins (or currants)**	**1 tbsp.**
3.	**Brown sugar, packed**	**2 tbsp.**
	Ground cinnamon	**⅛ tsp.**
4.	**Margarine**	**1 tsp.**
	Water	**3 tbsp.**

1. Wash the apples well. Remove the stems. Pierce down into the apples several times with the vegetable peeler, digging out as much of the core as possible. Peel a narrow strip around top of the apples. Place in the casserole.

2. Divide the raisins in half to fill the apple cavities.

3. Stir the brown sugar and cinnamon together in the cup. Press on top of the raisins. Sprinkle the remaining mixture over the apples.

4. Top each cavity with the margarine. Pour the water into the dish. Cover. Microwave on high (100%) for about 2 minutes. Microwave on medium (50%) for about 3 minutes until apples are fork tender, rotating dish ½ turn two times if you don't have a turntable. Let stand, covered, for 3 minutes. Spoon the juice over apples. Serves 2.

Made in the microwave, this is a great after-school snack for you and a friend.

Turtle Chocolates

GET READY ✔
2 heavy medium saucepans, measuring spoons, 2 long-handled mixing spoons, cookie sheet, waxed paper, dry measures, hot pad, table fork

1.	**Caramels**	**48**
	Milk	**3 tbsp.**
2.	**Chopped pecans**	**2 cups**
3.	**COATING**	
	Semisweet chocolate chips	**2 cups**

1. Unwrap the caramels and put them into one of the saucepans. Add the milk. Heat on low, stirring often, until the caramels are melted.

2. Cover the cookie sheet with the waxed paper. Grease the paper well. Add the pecans to the melted caramels. Stir. Leave on very low heat to keep from getting hard. Drop by rounded teaspoonfuls onto the waxed paper. Chill for 1 hour until firm.

3. **Coating:** Place the chocolate chips in the second saucepan. Heat on low, stirring often, until melted and smooth. Remove the saucepan to the hot pad. Drop 1 clump of caramel mixture at a time into the chocolate. Slide the fork under the piece and lift up to let the excess chocolate drip back into the saucepan. Repeat with the remaining pieces. Place back on the waxed paper. Chill. Makes 3 to 3½ dozen chocolates.

Left: Turtle Chocolates, above
Right: Marshmallow Delights, page 67

Marshmallow Delights

GET READY ✔

table knife, double boiler, dry measures, liquid measures, long-handled mixing spoon, hot pad, medium bowl, table fork, waxed paper

1.	Mackintosh's toffee bars (2 oz. each)	**3**
	Hard margarine	**¼ cup**
	Sweetened condensed milk	**⅔ cup**
2.	Special K cereal	**4 cups**
	Large white marshmallows	**30-35**

1. Break up the toffee bars by placing one bar in the palm of your hand. Hit the bar with the handle of the knife. Put the pieces into the top of the double boiler. Add the margarine and condensed milk. Put some hot water in the bottom of the double boiler. Set the top part in. Heat on medium-high, stirring occasionally, until melted and smooth. Remove the double boiler to the hot pad. Keep the toffee mixture over the hot water.

2. Measure the cereal into the bowl. Stick the fork into the end of one of the marshmallows. Roll the marshmallow in the toffee mixture to coat the bottom and sides. Hold the marshmallow over the toffee mixture to drain. Roll in the cereal, using your other hand to coat the bottom and sides. Push the marshmallow off of the fork. Place the uncoated end down onto the waxed paper. Repeat with the rest of the marshmallows. If the toffee mixture gets stiff, heat the water underneath until it begins to boil again. Makes 30 to 35 marshmallow treats.

Pictured on page 66.

Fiddle Diddles

GET READY ✔
dry measures, liquid measures, small saucepan, long-handled mixing spoon, hot pad, measuring spoons, small table spoon, large sheet of waxed paper, covered container

1.	Hard margarine	½ cup
	Granulated sugar	2 cups
	Milk	½ cup

2.	Cocoa powder	6 tbsp.
	Quick-cooking rolled oats (not instant)	3 cups
	Medium coconut	½ cup
	Chopped walnuts	½ cup
	Salt, just a pinch	
	Vanilla flavoring	1 tsp.

1. Put the margarine, sugar and milk into the saucepan. Heat on medium, stirring often, until the mixture comes to a boil. Remove the saucepan to the hot pad.

2. Add the remaining 6 ingredients. Stir well. Drop by rounded small table spoonfuls onto the waxed paper. Cool completely. Store, covered, in the container with waxed paper between the layers. Makes about 40 cookies.

Pictured below and on page 69.

A no-bake cookie that always turns out. Chocolate-flavored and nutty.

Fruity S'Mores

GET READY ✔
long-handled barbecue fork, small plate

1.	**Large white marshmallow**	**1**
2.	**Whole graham crackers**	**2**
	Squares of thin milk chocolate bar	**2-6**
	Thin slices of strawberry (or halves of seedless grapes)	**2**

1. Stick the fork in the end of the marshmallow, about ½ way through. Hold it over a fire or very hot burner until it is toasty brown and soft.

2. Place one of the graham cracker squares on the plate. Place the chocolate on the square. Push the marshmallow on top of the chocolate. Place the fruit slices on top of the marshmallow. Top with the second graham cracker. Push down, holding a few moments so the chocolate begins to melt. Makes 1 treat.

Left: Fruity S'Mores, above; Right: Fiddle Diddles, page 68

Fast. Easy. Looks fabulous! Tastes fabulous!

All Around S'Mores

GET READY ✓

table knife, small microwave-safe plate

1. **Round graham crackers**   **4**
    Hazelnut chocolate spread
    Large white or colored marshmallows   **2**

1. Use the knife to spread all 4 crackers with the chocolate spread. Place 2 of the crackers on the plate. Place the marshmallows on the top. Microwave on high (100%) for 15 seconds. Remove the plate from the microwave. Place the other 2 crackers on top of each marshmallow. Push down slightly until the marshmallows spread to the outer edges of the crackers. Makes 2 s'mores.

Variation 1: Use digestive biscuits or sugar cookies in place of the graham crackers.

Variation 2: Sprinkle chocolate chips or butterscotch chips on the bottom of 2 of the crackers. Microwave on high (100%) for 1 minute. Place the marshmallows on top. Microwave on high (100%) for 10 seconds. Top with the remaining crackers.

Choco Peanut Butter Dreams

GET READY ✔
liquid measures, medium bowl, electric mixer, dry measures, baking sheet, small table spoon, covered container

1. **Envelope of dessert topping (not prepared)** **1**
   Milk   **½ cup**

2. **Smooth peanut butter**   **½ cup**

3. **Milk**   **1 cup**
   Instant chocolate pudding powder   **1**
   (4 serving size)

4. **Package of chocolate wafers (about 48)**   **7 oz.**

1. Combine the dessert topping and first amount of milk in the bowl. Beat with the mixer on high speed until thickened.

2. Add the peanut butter. Beat on low speed until mixed.

3. Add the second amount of milk and pudding powder. Beat on low speed until blended. Beat on high speed for 2 minutes.

4. Place 24 of the wafers on the ungreased baking sheet. Put a heaping spoonful of the mixture on each wafer. Top with the remaining 24 wafers. Freeze, uncovered, for 3 hours. Put into the covered container to store. Makes 24 "dreams."

That wonderful combination of chocolate and peanut butter. A great treat to have in the freezer.

Have your friends help you make these—and then enjoy!

Coated Marshmallows

GET READY ✔
measuring spoons, small saucepan, liquid measures, dry measures, long-handled mixing spoon, hot pad, large bowl, table fork, waxed paper

1.	Hard margarine	1 tbsp.
	Golden corn syrup	⅔ cup
	Brown sugar, packed	⅓ cup
2.	Smooth peanut butter	½ cup
	Vanilla flavoring	½ tsp.
3.	Crisp rice cereal	5 cups
4.	Large white or colored marshmallows	24

1. Melt the margarine in the saucepan over medium. Add the corn syrup and brown sugar. Heat, stirring constantly, until boiling. Remove the saucepan to the hot pad.

2. Add the peanut butter. Stir until melted. Add the vanilla. Stir.

3. Put the cereal into the bowl.

4. Use the fork to dip each marshmallow into the peanut butter mixture until completely coated. Roll in the cereal. Set on the waxed paper to cool. Makes 24 marshmallows.

Recipe Index

Recipe Index 75

Feature Recipe from

Bag Lunches

Pick and pack your school lunch from this tasty collection of recipes for creative young cooks.

Butterscotch Pudding Cookies

GET READY ✔
measuring spoons, dry measures, medium bowl, mixing spoon, cookie sheet, table fork, oven mitts, wire rack, pancake lifter, waxed paper

1.	Hard margarine, melted	2 tbsp.
	Large egg, fork-beaten	1
	Instant butterscotch pudding powder (4 serving size)	1
	Biscuit mix	1 cup
	Milk	1 tbsp.

1. Place the oven rack in the center position. Turn the oven on to 350°F. Combine all 5 ingredients with the mixing spoon in the bowl. Shape the dough into balls, using 1 tbsp. dough for each. Place 3 inches apart on the ungreased cookie sheet. Make a crisscross pattern with the fork on top of each ball while lightly pressing down. Bake in the oven for 8 minutes. Use the oven mitts to remove the cookie sheet to the wire rack. Let stand for 2 minutes. Use the pancake lifter to remove the cookies to the waxed paper on the counter. Cool completely. Makes about 1½ dozen (18) cookies.

Variation: Add ½ cup chopped pecans or walnuts.

Cook's Notes